Spiritual

IMPARTATIONS BY GOD

DR. DONITA LESTER, MA, Ed. D. LPC

DR. DONITA LESTER, MA, Ed. D. LPC
Spiritual Impartations by God

Unless otherwise indicated, all Scripture quotations are taken from the King James Version and New International Version of the Bible.

Published work of:

All About You Consulting

ISBN-13: 978-0-578-84701-6

Dedication

This book is dedicated in *loving memory* of my mother Evone Lamar Lester and my father Richard Lee Lester.

The both of you have gone on to be with the Lord. And without God's use of you, to bring me into this world, I would not be here.

Momma, you are the one that taught me the importance of prayer, reading God's word, and living a Holy life. I love you and miss you, momma.

Daddy, you had so much swag. I'd like to think that you are the one that left me with class and style.

I am a woman of elegance because of both of you. I love you and miss both of you dearly.

Dr. Donita Lester's Journey

My journey with Christ started at the age of 16 and to God be the glory, I am now (at the time of releasing this book) 54 years of age. My recollections of how I came to know God began as a little girl being trained by the example of my mother, Evone Lamar Lester, who has since gone on to be with the Lord.

My mother lived by the following scripture, "Train up a child in the way he should go: and when he is old, he will not depart from it" (Proverbs 22:6 KJV). I remember my mother taking me and my siblings to church, whether we wanted to go or not. Going to Sunday morning worship was just one of the services that led to Bible class on Wednesday nights and Friday night services. Then we added to the agenda what is known as shut-ins in the church. During these shut-in services, I learned how to travail and intercede in prayer all night long. We sang, prayed, read scripture, testified, and waited to hear from the Lord. During these times, deliverance of all sorts took place. The saints of God prayed until they saw manifested change in the lives of people. Those were the good old days! The power of God was so great in the room that it looked foggy!

As I reflect on things now, I can see how my mother demonstrated to my siblings and me the importance of attendance in the house of God. I was raised in a Pentecostal church named Lively Stone Church of God in St. Louis, Missouri. There I was baptized in Jesus' name and received that gift of the Holy Ghost according to Acts 2:4 (KJV) where it states, "And they were all filled with the Holy Ghost, and began to speak with other tongues, as the Spirit gave them utterance." I also was raised with the following belief, "That if thou shalt confess with thy mouth the Lord Jesus, and shalt believe in thine heart that God hath raised him from the dead, thou shalt be saved" (Romans 10:9, KJV).

At the time of releasing this book, I am a member of New Life Covenant Church Southeast, in Chicago Illinois.

After very early in my salvation, I remember being separated from the world by God to do a work for Him. I learned what it meant to walk with God and to serve Him. I participated as a leader of testimony service along with leading high praise services in my church. From there I served as a missionary in prayer with people that desired to receive more of God and would eventually pray with them in what we call the prayer room.

Soon after, I felt the call on my life to do more and I eventually answered the call to be an evangelist, to preach and teach God's word. In this capacity I served in prison ministry, street ministry, taught Sunday school, and developed a radio broadcast ministry called God Cares Ministries. Today, I continue to serve God and await His continued instruction and direction for my life.

TABLE OF CONTENTS

DAY ONE - BELIEVE TO SEE.. 1

DAY TWO - LIVING IN THE FLOW OF YES............... 5

DAY THREE - THE LOVE ACT 8

DAY FOUR - ARE YOU STILL ANTICIPATING?..... 12

DAY FIVE - A LIFE POURED OUT 15

DAY SIX - THE SUN REFUSED TO SHINE BECAUSE

OF THE SON 18

DAY SEVEN - WHAT IS SUCCESS?............................ 22

DAY EIGHT - WHAT KIND OF LOVE IS THIS? 25

DAY NINE - TOUCHED BY OUR FEELINGS............. 28

DAY TEN - OPEN MY EYES 31

DAY ELEVEN - OPEN MY EARS.................................. 35

DAY TWELVE - HIS THOUGHTS 38

DAY THIRTEEN - MY FRIEND 41

DAY FOURTEEN - NOT IN A HURRY 44

DAY FIFTEEN - PUSH 47

DAY SIXTEEN - PERFECT PEACE............................. 51

DAY SEVENTEEN - SERVE THE LORD WITH GLADNESS 54

DAY EIGHTEEN - WHEN GOD SEEMS FAR AWAY 57

DAY NINETEEN - TRUSTING GOD WHEN YOU CAN'T TRACE HIM 61

DAY TWENTY - WAIT FOR HIM 65

DAY TWENTY-ONE - BE STILL AND KNOW 70

DAY TWENTY-TWO - THE VOICE OF GOD 74

DAY TWENTY-THREE - WALK WORTHY 77

DAY TWENTY-FOUR - BE NOT WEARY 81

DAY TWENTY-FIVE - WHAT GOD ALLOWS 85

DAY TWENTY-SIX - RENEW YOUR MIND 88

DAY TWENTY-SEVEN - ORDER MY STEPS 94

DAY TWENTY-EIGHT - HOW TO PROSPER 98

DAY TWENTY-NINE - THAT I MIGHT KNOW HIM 102

DAY THIRTY - PRAISE HIM 105

DAY ONE - BELIEVE TO SEE

There are times in our lives when things appear to be a blur. Our vision concerning Gods' plan for our lives may be obscure. Maybe there will be a trial that we'll face and perhaps it will be the longevity of the tribulations we'll experience. Whatever your situation is please know that it is okay to tell God about it. Your life is in His hands. Before the foundation of the world, He knew exactly how you would feel in these different moments.

Perhaps you think no one could possibly know what it is like to be where you are. Let me assure you that it's quite the contrary. Hebrews 4:15 says, "For we do not have a High Priest who cannot sympathize with our weaknesses but was in all points tempted as we are, yet without sin" (NKJV). What this means for you is that God truly understands where you are and what you're going through. God will show you compassion. You only need to come to Him.

1

To give ourselves another example of a person who can relate to hard trials and tribulations we can look at the life of David. He was a man who was known to go through great trials. While his story is written in many books of the Bible, one great example could be the anguish he proclaimed in Psalms 27:13-14. David cried out to the Lord and reminded God of some things. David found the strength he needed as he communed with God. It was during his difficulties that he poured out his true feelings and thoughts to God. Ultimately, David concluded that he would wait on God. He believed to see the salvation of the Lord in his life. Somewhere during his prayer, he resolved within himself that he would believe God! He concluded that he would see the goodness of the Lord in the land of the living!

We must do as he did and declare, "I will see the goodness of the Lord in the land of the living!" David made it clear that there were things he would see while he still resided on earth. I reiterate on earth, not when he got to heaven. This means no matter what, it's going to happen in your lifetime. It's going to happen for you! I encourage you to believe to see. Believe that you will see the goodness of the Lord while you live, move, and have your being here on earth.

DAY ONE JOURNALING

_____

_____

_____

_____

_____

_____

_____

_____

_____

_____

_____

_____

_____

_____

"I had fainted, unless I had believed to see the goodness of the LORD in the land of the living." Psalm 27:13 KJV

DAY TWO - LIVING IN THE FLOW OF YES

There are many things that people seek on a daily basis. Some seek money, fame, fortune, prosperity, and much more. What are you seeking? I am compelled to say that only when you seek what Christ has for you, will your desires come to pass. Take a moment and think about it. Are you really seeking ALL that God has promised you? According to 2 Corinthians 1:20, "For all the promises of God in Him are YES, and in Him Amen, to the glory of God through us" (NKJV). Look closely at this scripture. In Him is YES and in Him is AMEN. When you seek all that He has for you He will affirm things. This is the meaning of *yes*. In Him is amen. Amen means *so be it.*

Additionally, another portion of that verse speaks of the glory of God through us. This means that God wants glory out of us. God wants glory out of what you attain. God gets glory through and from His yes to you. God gets glory out of your yes to Him. How powerful is that?! The *yes* belongs to God and the *yes* belongs to you. It's yours because He gave it to you. It's His because He gave it to you. What am I saying? I am saying that everything you have, God gave it to you. You have nothing in and apart from Him. In Acts 17:28 it says, "Herein is the core of our existence. For in Him we live and move and have our being. As some of your own poets have said, we are His offspring" (NIV).

Living in the flow of yes means to always examine ourselves and the posture of our prayers. Do you have unanswered prayers? Has God told you no about something that you prayed for? Are you still waiting for something to happen? Perhaps your requests are out of line with His divine promises for your life. You can get your prayers answered. This is the confidence we have in approaching God: that if we ask anything according to His will, He hears us (I John 5:14 NLT). Think about this. What if He turned your NO into a YES?!

DAY TWO JOURNALING

_____

_____

_____

_____

_____

_____

_____

_____

_____

_____

_____

_____

_____

_____

_____

_____

"For all the promises of God in Him are yes, and in Him amen, to the glory of God through us." 2 Corinthians 1:20 NKJV

DAY THREE - THE LOVE ACT

What kind of love is this? In John 15:13 it says, "Greater love hath no one than this, that a man lay down his life for his friends." This love that Christ is referring to is a *selfless act of love* also known as *agape love*. Our Lord and Savior Jesus Christ was thinking of you and me when He displayed this love on the cross. For some, this may be hard to grasp. It may be hard to imagine. Like really, how did Jesus lay down His life for you and me? What was this process like? How and why would He do such a thing? John 3:16 gives us the *why* answer. It explains, "For God so loved the world that he gave his only begotten Son, that whosoever believeth in him should not perish, but have everlasting life."

The *process* is explained in Hebrews 2:14-18. In this text, it basically explains that we, His children, are human beings and because of this, He (God) became a human in the person of Jesus Christ. The text further explains that *only* as a human being could He die. Don't forget He is a spirit. He literally became like us so that we could become like Him. He put on *human flesh* to identify with what comes with the fleshly experience. Some might be thinking, but doesn't He know all things? Yes! He's omniscient, which means he's all-knowing. However, when He took on human flesh it allowed Him to experience what we go through in our flesh. Check out Hebrews 4:15. Jesus became our high priest, going to God on our behalf. He became the ultimate sacrifice for us. He was tempted like as we, yet without sin. The difference is that we inherited the sinful nature of Adam, making us prone to sin.

The explanation of His death allows us to know that His death was not in vain. It was to break the power of the devil who had the power of death. How? You may ask. According to Romans 5:12, when Adam sinned, sin entered the world. Adam's sin brought death, so death spread to everyone, for everyone sinned. I reiterate according to scripture that only by dying in this way could He set free all

who have lived their lives as slaves to the fear of dying.

God's plan for us surpasses our finite minds. You can now

live free from the penalty of sin. Remember the Love Act!

DAY THREE JOURNALING

_____

_____

_____

_____

_____

_____

_____

_____

_____

_____

_____

_____

_____

_____

_____

"Greater love hath no one than this that a man lay down his life for his friends." John 15:13 KJV

DAY FOUR - ARE YOU STILL ANTICIPATING?

The word for the day is *anticipation*! What are you anticipating? Anticipation means to expect or predict. Did you know you can live with expectancy? The scripture states, "My soul, wait in silence for God alone, for my expectation is from him" (Psalm 62:5 NHEB). In your stillness wait for Him! Live your life with expectancy from God alone. This will prevent disappointment in people. You can depend on Him. He will come through!

While you wait, I encourage you to wait with a praise. Wait with the thought of *He's going do everything that He promises me.* Wait on Him knowing that He has not forgotten you. Think about who made you the promise. God is not a man that He should lie, nor the son of man that He should repent. Has He said, and will He not do it? Or has He spoken, and will He not make it good? (Numbers 23:19)

You can predict your future. Start saying what you want to see. *Say what you see, so you can see what you say.* In Proverbs 18:21 it states, "Death and life are in the power of the tongue: and they that love it shall eat the fruit thereof." The predictions of your life can be your reality. One caution in all of this is to make sure your heart is in the right place. This is what God looks at. Take a look at the scriptures that deal with matters of the heart. I have a few I can provide for you: Proverbs 23:7; Luke 6:45; and Proverbs 4:23. Keep anticipating and know that your expectancy is from the Lord!

DAY FOUR JOURNALING

_____

_____

_____

_____

_____

_____

_____

_____

_____

_____

_____

_____

_____

_____

_____

_____

"My soul, wait in silence for God alone, for my expectation is from Him." Psalm 62:5 NHEB

DAY FIVE - A LIFE POURED OUT

I can change the world! You can change the world! We can change the world! Philippians 4:13 says, "I can do all things through Christ who strengthens me" (NKJV). Will you join me? I want to live a life poured out! Not sure if you've noticed but this is my sign-off in every post you've read from me – if you've followed me on social media. *A life poured out.* What does this mean? It means to empty yourself of all that God has given you. What has God given you? What can you give back to Him?

Amazing how everything you have is given, inspired, generated, prompted, and orchestrated by God. Think about it. What do you have internally or externally that you weren't given by God? Check out what Job 1:21 says, "I came naked from my mother's womb, and I will be naked when I leave. The LORD gave me what I had, and the LORD has taken it away. Praise the name of the LORD!" (NLT) What's really important is that you have an appointment that is certain. In Hebrews 9:27 it states, "And it is appointed unto men once to die, but after this the judgment." This is a truth that we should embrace. It can no doubt be scary at times for some to embrace. Nonetheless, it is certain. Spend your days pouring out. Discipline yourself into how you can really give back to God in every area of your life. Don't miss your moment! There should be an urgency in your spirit that says, *Lord, I want to please you!* When it's all said and done, only what we do for Christ will last.

My prayer is that you will find pleasure in pouring out. I pray that you place more emphasis on the purpose given to you by our creator. He is our LORD! He is our SAVIOR! He is the SON of the MOST HIGH! HE is JESUS CHRIST!!! May God richly bless you! Please share this with others.

DAY FIVE JOURNALING

_____

_____

_____

_____

_____

_____

_____

_____

_____

_____

_____

_____

_____

_____

_____

_____

"I can do all things through Christ who strengthens me."
Philippians 4:13 NKJV

DAY SIX - THE SUN REFUSED TO SHINE BECAUSE OF THE SON

At the time of writing this journal, this day was a pretty spectacular day for the world! It was a time where the day was turned to night. It was a time that some described as "Darkness has fallen!" Reporter David Muir with *World News* said, "If you can see the sun you're about to see nighttime." He further shared, "It's a once in a lifetime moment." Yet another reporter stated, "We have gone into complete darkness!" I'm speaking of the phenomenon of the total solar eclipse that spanned across the United States on August 21, 2017.

Awestruck we all were! We witnessed the earth, the moon, and the sun in a way that many had not ever experienced in their lifetime. It was the moment that many had been waiting for! Some were ecstatic! Many described it as amazing! Some have said, "I'm still feeling it now!" It was described as being seen in totality. Some reporters became emotional while reporting the phenomena. One reporter stated, "It really puts us in our place." Some described it as spiritual.

If you had the opportunity to witness this event, what was your response? My response was, "Wow! Look at God!" There is a time in scripture that we see this same type of response from the sun and moon. The scripture tells us at Matthew 27:45, "At noon, darkness fell across the whole land until three o'clock." The solar event of 2017 mimics what happened on the cross when Jesus died. The sun and the moon refused to shine. I can't help but think, what if God did not allow the sun to shine anymore? I think about how this phenomenon disrupted nature. It definitely had an effect on the animals. They all responded in confusion because the atmosphere changed.

Walk with me for a moment. This was a God event! The reactions and responses from God's creation (i.e., men, women, children, and animals) were a clear indication that we all understood that this was something beyond humanity. Let's take it a step further and look at how darkness affects our climate. The reporters stated that the temperature even changed. No one could deny that this was an amazing moment in time. Isn't it equally as amazing that this response is not shown when we speak of the coming of our Lord? After all, isn't He the reason for the sun and the moon being in existence? He's the one that decided how the earth would receive light and darkness. Perhaps we'd get a better response if we could predict the coming of the Lord. Remember, the sun refused to shine because of the Son!

DAY SIX JOURNALING

_____

_____

_____

_____

_____

_____

_____

_____

_____

_____

_____

_____

_____

_____

_____

"From noon, until three in afternoon darkness came over all of the land." Matthew 27:45 NIV

DAY SEVEN - WHAT IS SUCCESS?

Like words, success means many different things to many different people. According to Webster's Dictionary, the meaning of success is the accomplishment of an aim or purpose. Perhaps your reflections of where you are and what you hoped you'd be doing don't match. Maybe you feel you should be further along in your career. Is there a promotion you thought you should have by now?

Often, we think of success and look at our own and can become doubtful of the path we're on. But we must ask ourselves, what makes us successful? Whose standard are we measuring our success against?

What I love about God is that He always comes to counter the world's definition of a thing. In Joshua 1:7-8, God is speaking to Joshua after the leader Moses dies and after the children of Israel have been wandering in the wilderness for forty years. God is now ready to give them the land He'd

22

promised them. He was ready to take them over the Jordan River. Where is God ready to take you? Don't you want to see the land God wants to give you? I hear you saying, *Yes! Yes, God! I am ready to see my Promised Land!*

Okay, all you have to do is obey *all* that God has spoken to you. All you have to do is meditate day and night in His word to be certain you are on the right track about what He's telling you to do. Don't forget to obey the instructions of your leader. Be certain to meditate on His word day and night. Don't deviate from what you know God has said to you. Then and only then will you prosper and succeed in all you do.

DAY SEVEN JOURNALING

_____

_____

_____

_____

_____

_____

_____

_____

_____

_____

_____

_____

_____

"...For then thou shalt make thy way prosperous, and then thou shalt have good success." Joshua 1:8 KJV

DAY EIGHT - WHAT KIND OF LOVE IS THIS?

Lord, I want to love like you. Have you ever thought you were in love? Maybe you thought someone loved you until the toughness of life came and they left. Someone promised you that you could count on them. They promised for better or worse they'd be with you. You quickly learned it was quite the contrary. The scripture says in St. John 3:16, "For God so loved the world that He gave His only begotten son that whosoever believeth in Him should not perish but have everlasting life." This is real love. God's love is the kind of love that gives *His only…* What are you willing to give? God's love is the kind of love that endures. God's love is the kind of love that looks beyond your faults and sees your need. God's love is the greatest love in the world!

No one can compete with it. No one can compare. You can trust Him completely. His love remains. He's been faithful and will always show up. You can count on His love.

He's consistent. His love, it never fails, and it never gives up. Though the seasons change His love remains. According to scripture, "Greater love hath no one than this, that a man lay down His life for His friends" (St. John 15:13 KJV). God sent His Son to lay down His life for you. He calls you friend. While we were yet sinners, He loved us. His love is unconditional. It's not based on anything you can do. When we were far apart from Him. He came running with open arms. Jesus Christ was and is a perfect example of what real love looks like. What kind of love is this?

DAY EIGHT JOURNALING

_____

_____

_____

_____

_____

_____

_____

_____

_____

_____

_____

_____

_____

_____

"For God so loved the world that He gave His only begotten Son, that whoever believes in Him should not perish but have everlasting life." St. John 3:16 NKJV

DAY NINE - TOUCHED BY OUR FEELINGS

I want to feel what you feel. God is touched by what we feel. He has experienced, in every way, exactly what you feel now, in your past, and in your future. Can you believe it? You are not alone. No matter how stupid, silly, ridiculous, absurd, and any other word that describes how you may be feeling, He knows about it. Here's the awesome aspect of His knowledge. He knows the height of your feelings. This means from the crown of your head to the soles of your feet - He knows about it. He understands the width. This means He knows the extent of your feelings.

Further, our Lord and Savior Jesus Christ knows the areas of your life to which your feelings consume you. How amazing! It doesn't stop there because He knows the depth of your feelings. This means He knows how complex your feelings are. He is aware. In His word, you can find comfort. This High Priest of ours understands our weaknesses, for He faced all the testing that we experience, yet He did not sin (Hebrews 4:15 NLT). Your savior put on humanity so that He would know exactly what the flesh of man would experience. He went to this extent to fully know your human experience. Ultimately, He became like us so that we could become like Him. What a mighty God we serve!

DAY NINE JOURNALING

_____

_____

_____

_____

_____

_____

_____

_____

_____

_____

_____

_____

_____

_____

"For we have not an high priest which cannot be touched with the feeling of our infirmities." Hebrews 4:15 KJV

DAY TEN - OPEN MY EYES

I want to see what you see. In your walk with God, it is imperative that you comprehend and be well informed about all spiritual matters concerning God's will for your life. "I ask that the eyes of your heart be enlightened, in order for you to know what is the hope of His calling, what are the riches of the glory of His inheritance in the saints" (Ephesians 1:18). God wants you to know that you were once separated from Him but now you have hope because of Christ dying on the cross. It means that no matter what you are faced with you have hope. Lamentations 3:21 (KJV) states. "This I recall to my mind, therefore I have hope." This is what will sustain you as you face the trials and tribulations of this life.

Still, there's more! God has riches for us that we inherited because He sent His only begotten son into the world, that the world through Him might be saved.

Specifically, those who accept Him as their Savior will reap the benefits of the inheritance. There are things we inherited that we'll experience on earth, and some will ultimately happen in glory. Think of it this way. Someone died and left you something. What would you do? You would first and foremost find out who that someone is. You would then find out what you needed to do to pick up what had been left to you. Once you determine whom you need to contact, what you need to do, when you could meet the person, and where to go - you would be on your way. Right? Certainly, you would!

This is precisely the same thing you need to do where God's inheritance for you is concerned. You must get busy trying to figure out what has been left for you by Jesus Christ. Maybe you don't know where to begin. Just start with getting into a good Bible-based community where you can learn the word of God through the teaching of the gospel. Also, begin talking with God in prayer. In prayer ask God to reveal His word to you and I am certain He will do that for you. Don't forget you have an inheritance awaiting you!

DAY TEN JOURNALING

_____

_____

_____

_____

_____

_____

_____

_____

_____

_____

_____

_____

"I pray that the eyes of your heart may be enlightened, so that you will know what is the hope of His calling, what are the riches of the glory of His inheritance in the saints." Ephesians 1:18 NASB

DAY ELEVEN - OPEN MY EARS

Tell me what you heard. He has something He wants to share with you. What did God say? Did you notice He's speaking? In the book of Isaiah 55:6-7 (KJV) is states, "Seek the Lord while He may be found, call upon Him while He is near. Let the wicked forsake his way and the unrighteous man his thoughts; let him return to the Lord, and He will have mercy on him; and our God, for He will abundantly pardon."

God has given you a summons through an invitation to seek Him. He's honest with you about the fact that He will not always be near. He even shares the details and conditions of how you should approach Him. The specifics are that you must leave some ways and thoughts behind in order to approach Him. He recognizes that you once sought Him (return back unto him). He makes it clear the benefits of returning. Simply, He will forgive you no matter what it

35

is. And He has plenty of forgiveness to cover your past, present, and future. He puts them in the sea of forgetfulness. Someone said, "He has a sea that doesn't have the ability to remember." Say to the Lord, I'm learning to listen. I want to rest in your nearness. I'm starting to notice You are speaking.

DAY ELEVEN JOURNALING

_____

_____

_____

_____

_____

_____

_____

_____

_____

_____

_____

_____

_____

"Seek the Lord while He may be found, call upon Him while He is near. Let the wicked forsake his way and the unrighteous man his thoughts; let him return to the Lord, and He will have mercy on him; and our God, for He will abundantly pardon."
Isaiah 55:6-7 KJV

DAY TWELVE - HIS THOUGHTS

Tell me your thoughts while they're on your mind. It's high time to know His thoughts. It's really true that God does not think as we do. His thoughts go beyond our wildest dreams and imaginations. When we elevate our thinking to the place where He is, therein is an invitation to abundant living. Isaiah 55:8 (KJV) says, "For My thoughts are not your thoughts, nor are your ways my ways," says the Lord. Simply put, when God thinks a thing, it is. When His thoughts are spoken, they materialize. Ask Him to tell you His thoughts. He will.

If you notice He says, "His ways are not are ways". It means the way He does things is different from ours. His ways are higher because of who He is. There is a certain level He desires for His people to live on. You wonder how this could be and how it's even possible. It's possible because in God you have a strength that is under His control.

Philippians 4:13 (KJV) says, "I can do all things through Christ who strengthens me." In Him is all you need. Through the word of God, it is truly possible to know His ways and thoughts.

DAY TWELVE JOURNALING

_____

_____

_____

_____

_____

_____

_____

_____

_____

_____

_____

_____

"For My thoughts are not your thoughts, nor are your ways my ways, says the Lord." Isaiah 55:8 KJV

DAY THIRTEEN - MY FRIEND

I'll be your friend. God calls you friend. Have you accepted Him as your Lord and Savior? Did you speak to Him today? I encourage you to do so. He didn't want heaven without you. So, He brought heaven to you. He thought of you before the foundation of the world. Greater love has no one than this, that a man lay down his life for his friends (St. John 15:13 KJV). He proved His love for you when He died upon the cross. This was a major event. He shed His blood and took upon Himself everything that He knew you would face in your past, present, and future. What a friend!

How will you respond to what's been done for you? Will you ignore the price that's been paid? When you do nothing with what you have heard, you've chosen. He is patiently awaiting your reply. Think of it as a gift that costs you nothing. What do you say when someone takes the time to pick you out a gift and bring it to your house? This is what Christ has done for you. He's expecting you to respond to Him with your life. He is saying, come! Come, is an invitation to a party where all things have been made ready. Will you show up at the party? There's a seat at the table with your name on it. Put on your best apparel with your fineries. It's an extravaganza!

DAY THIRTEEN JOURNALING

_____

_____

_____

_____

_____

_____

_____

_____

_____

_____

_____

_____

_____

_____

_____

"Greater love hath no one than this, that a man lay down his life for his friends." John 15:13 KJV

DAY FOURTEEN - NOT IN A HURRY

I don't want to rush ahead. Sometimes we get ahead of God. It means that there are times when we feel like God is taking too long. Or maybe you think that God has forgotten about you. The only thing that is certain is that God cannot lie. If He did not keep His word, do you know what that would mean for the Body of Christ? He would cease being God. It means that He is not trustworthy. It would make Him a liar. "God is not a man that he should lie; neither the son of man that He should repent: hath He said, and shall He not do it? Or hath He spoken, and shall He not make it good?" (Numbers 23:19).

Wait for God's timing. Let me assure you that it will happen. The scripture says, "For the vision is yet for an appointed time and it hastens to the end [fulfillment]; it will not deceive or disappoint. Though it tarry, wait [earnestly] for it, because it will surely come; it will not be behind on its appointed day" (Habakkuk 2:3 NIV). He has not forgotten what He said. You see, there is a time and season for everything under heaven. Just as it's certain that our climate changes every year from winter, fall, spring, and summer the same holds true for the seasons in your life. According to the word of God we read that "To everything there is a season, and a time to every purpose under the heaven" (Ecclesiastes 3:1 KJV). Your responsibility when it comes to God's promises for you is that you continue believing, as well as trusting, in His promises. They are always *yes* and *amen*! (2 Corinthians 1:20 KJV).

DAY FOURTEEN JOURNALING

_____

_____

_____

_____

_____

_____

_____

_____

_____

_____

_____

_____

"For the vision is yet for an appointed time and it hastens to the end [fulfillment]; it will not deceive or disappoint. Though it tarry, wait [earnestly] for it, because it will surely come; it will not be behind on its appointed day." Habakkuk 2:3 NIV

DAY FIFTEEN - PUSH

How do we see manifestation of our prayers? We must pray until something happens! It means that you need more than persistence. For God has given us the authority to approach His throne. We must approach His thrown confidently, knowing that all of what we've faced is known by God. You can, with certainty, approach Him knowing He understands you better than you understand yourself. The scripture says, "Let us therefore come boldly unto the throne of grace, that we may obtain mercy, and find grace to help in time of need" (Hebrews 4:16). Note that therefore means 'because of something' or 'for that reason' you can come. It's because of the unmerited favor of God. You can come because He hung, bled, and died for you. This is precisely why you can approach Him.

Still, manifestation comes when we put Him in remembrance of His word. Check out what your heavenly

Father says. He says, "Put Me in remembrance [remind Me of your merits]; let us plead *and* argue together. Set forth your case, that you may be justified (proved right)" (Isaiah 43:26 AMPC).

Particularly, He's saying tell me how you qualify for what you're asking of me. Tell me how you are even worthy of what you press me about. Bring to my attention how this is even right for you. It means with all of your might tell me about it! He's saying give me some concrete facts about this request.

Afterward, when you've done this, watch Him do it! I hear a hastening to perform in your life what He's spoken unto you. You will hear the Lord say, "Then said the LORD unto me, Thou hast well seen: for I will hasten my word to perform it" (Jeremiah 1:12 KJV).

Finally, be assured that He's waiting to perform His word in your life! His words, they are spirit, and they are life!

He remains able through His word to allow you to see a performance (John 6:63). His words can induce (bring about) and compel (force) powerful reactions in your life. He even has angels that are waiting to do His biddings (Psalm 103:20).

DAY FIFTEEN JOURNALING

_____

_____

_____

_____

_____

_____

_____

_____

_____

_____

_____

_____

_____

*"Let us therefore come boldly unto the throne of grace, that
we may obtain mercy, and find grace to help in time of need."
Hebrews 4:16 KJV*

DAY SIXTEEN - PERFECT PEACE

The peace of God is perfect. Having God's peace means that you don't have disturbance in anything or with anything that is going on in life. Notice what Isaiah 26:3 (KJV) says, "Thou wilt keep him in perfect peace, whose mind is stayed on thee: because he trusteth in thee." This is the kind of peace God wants you to have. Why does He give this type of peace? Why should you have it? God does this because He wants you to have the ability to identify when the peace is from Him and when it's not.

For example, there is false peace; there is temporary peace; and there is tainted peace to name a few. The peace that comes from God is flawless. It's the kind of peace that is both sprinkled and saturated in the elements of His character. It gives you the ability to elude (escape) all negativities. It's the kind of peace that transcends life circumstances. It is this kind of peace that regulates your mind, soul, and body when faced with difficulties and challenges.

Another amazing thought about God's peace is that it can continue as long as your mind remains on Him. You see, having the peace of God means that transformation has to take place in your mind. You must train yourself to think like Christ. "Let this mind be in you, which was also in Christ Jesus" (Philippians 2:5 KJV). This can be done by reading God's word for His instruction. This comes with time and experience with God. Now that you've done this, it's evidence to God that you trust Him. It shows Him that you have faith in what He has made available to you through and by His (Jesus') shed blood. May you use the peace that God gives you in every area of your life!

DAY SIXTEEN JOURNALING

_____

_____

_____

_____

_____

_____

_____

_____

_____

_____

_____

_____

_____

_____

_____

"Thou wilt keep him in perfect peace, whose mind is stayed on thee: because he trusteth in thee." Isaiah 26:3 KJV

DAY SEVENTEEN - SERVE THE LORD WITH GLADNESS

What we do for Christ should be done in the right posture. There is a certain attitude that goes with living for Him. In our walk with Him, we should never become stale. What we present to God should have a sweet-smelling savor. Others should desire to know who this God is that we profess to serve. We are told in scripture to, "Serve the LORD with gladness: come before His presence with singing" (Psalm 100:2 KJV).

The gladness that is mentioned here means you are delighted to do what you do for Him with great pleasure! It is both an honor and privilege to be chosen by Him. Remember, you did not choose Him, He chose you. We can't deny that walking with Christ brings about its own challenges. However, we can admit that what Jesus Christ did for us is far more than we can ever do for Him. We could never repay Him. Thereby, our struggles cannot compare to His.

Now you can sing before the presence of God with joy and gladness. Singing represents a way to praise Him and give Him glory while you are in His presence. Tell yourself, I will sing because I am happy! I will sing because I am free! Praise the Lord, I am free! To God be the glory for the things He has done! What a faithful and mighty God we serve!

DAY SEVENTEEN JOURNALING

_____

_____

_____

_____

_____

_____

_____

_____

_____

_____

_____

_____

_____

_____

_____

_____

"Serve the LORD with gladness: come before His presence with singing." Psalm 100:2 KJV

DAY EIGHTEEN - WHEN GOD SEEMS FAR AWAY

There are times when God seems far away. He has closed the distance between us and Him through the blood of Jesus Christ. We all have had those thoughts at one time or another on this journey. God is in our story. He's closer than the breath we breathe. Deuteronomy 30:14 says, "But the word is very near you, in your mouth and in your heart, that you may observe it." The important thing to remember is that you can simply speak the word and it will change things for you. The power of life and death is in the tongue. In other words, say what you see, so you can see what you say.

Sometimes it's the way you are living your life. It's not until you begin to seek Him that you will find Him. According to Jeremiah 29:13, "And ye shall seek me, and find me, when ye shall search for me with all your heart." In another portion of scripture, He has said, "If you draw nigh to me, I will draw nigh to you" (James 4:8). While we were yet sinners, He loved us! So, don't let anything stand between you and the Father. No matter what you did and where you are He wants a relationship with you. How awesome is that?! God has broken the rules for you.

I want to give you another perspective about the nearness of God. In the book of John, chapter four, there is a story about a Samaritan woman at Jacob's Well. Keep in mind that the culture of that time did not allow Jews to share things in common with Samaritans. This will help you understand the response of the women at the well. This woman came to a place to draw natural water. This lady had an earthly perspective. But, this lady had an appointment with the Living Water (Jesus) and did not know it. The moral of the story is that you may come and drink from the well (Jesus) that never runs dry.

You see, God knows the truth about you, and He still wants fellowship with you. Yes, you! He wants you to get to know Him. Jesus has need of you. All you have to do is say yes! He knows everything about you, and He still likes you. In fact, He loves you. All He wants you to know is that He is looking at you through His holy binoculars. He wants you to come to Him in truth. He desires truth in the (inward) parts according to Psalm 51:6. Be willing to worship Him in spirit, His spirit. In the spirit of the truth of who you are. Take hold of His will. Jesus Christ, in Him alone the work will be done in you. This is His heavenly perspective about you! He's closer than you think. Always remember that God will never leave you nor will He forsake you (Hebrews 13:5). Whenever you feel distant from God it's because you've stepped away not Him. He keeps His promises, and He is consistent in all His ways. He will always be with you, even until the end of the world (Isaiah 41:10).

DAY EIGHTEEN JOURNALING

_____

_____

_____

_____

_____

_____

_____

_____

_____

_____

_____

_____

_____

_____

"...I will never leave us nor forsake thee." Hebrews 13:5 NIV

DAY NINETEEN - TRUSTING GOD WHEN YOU CAN'T TRACE HIM

Trust is the principal thing. This is asked of you by God. But how do you trust what you can't see? And how do you trust whom you've never touched in a tangible way? The reason this becomes a challenge for humanity is because God is a spirit and cannot be seen with the natural eye. Do you believe seeing is believing? Here's what the scripture says, "Jesus saith unto him, Thomas, because thou hast seen me, thou hast believed: blessed *are* they that have not seen, and *yet* have believed" (John 20:29 KJV). Detection of Him must be revealed by Him. God has to choose to reveal Himself. You have to receive him, or you have no revelation of Him. He is outside our cognitive and intellectual abilities. So, how do you trust then? What is trust?

Trust is an action word that means firm belief in the reliability, truth, ability, or strength of someone or something. This description of what trust means says that you can't guess about it. This task comes through an experience facilitated by a relationship. One can only know reliability, ability, and or/truth through encounters with the person. So, what encounters have you personally had with God? Once you reflect on it, determine whether or not He came through for you. With your experience, did you find Him to be untruthful? Did He show up for you? Did He prove Himself to be faithful? What is God's track record in your life? Is He able?

Still, faith is another very important factor when it comes to trusting God. Faith and trust work simultaneously. Faith is complete trust or confidence in someone or something. This exercise works when you are connected to God. You can say you trust God. However, it would be virtually impossible to trust Him and have no assurance that there will be results. You must know you can count on Him. We do not serve a God that sometimes shows up. We don't have an absentee God! He is consistent, faithful, willing, and able. He is God. Recite this to yourself: *God knows what I need, when I need it, and how to get it to me.* Let your ears hear these words come out of your mouth. Faith comes by hearing and hearing by the word of God (Romans 10:17).

DAY NINETEEN JOURNALING

_____

_____

_____

_____

_____

_____

_____

_____

_____

_____

_____

_____

"Jesus saith unto him, Thomas, because thou hast seen me, thou hast believed: blessed are they that have not seen, and yet have believed." John 20:29 KJV

DAY TWENTY - WAIT FOR HIM

Waiting for God can sometimes mean becoming comfortable in an uncomfortable circumstance. The question then becomes why do we have to wait on God when He can just do what I am asking for? The best way to wait on God is to wait on Him with a praise. Your mindset has to be that I will not let my circumstances determine my response. Can you wait without a sign?

We can't sit in despair and despondency. We must look at the right reason for waiting. Your circumstance does not determine whether God is going to do it. You don't let your circumstance dictate your response. You let your God tell your circumstance what will be. You must have hope to wait on what you don't have now. You must resolve that you don't have to have it now if it's not what God wants you to have. I'd rather wait for the best God has, wouldn't you? The elements that you need in your waiting are hope and promise. Your hope must remain in place in order to receive the promises of God. God's promises are yes and amen! With this, you can know that He will do what He says. You must give Him glory and wait for it to come to pass.

Your attitude must be *I am looking for the best. I am expecting the best. I will not stop looking for it.* Don't let the devil make you think it won't come to pass. Don't stop demanding the best. And don't stop being the best. Any time you stop hoping you are saying God won't deliver. You have to emphatically state, in spite of where you are right now, my God delivers!

The problem is that you have begun to ask how. How am I going to get out of this? *How* cannot be your focus, God is responsible for your how. Frankly, it's His business. Continue to wait. This is now faith. Having expectation is a key part of faith. Wait means something is going to happen here. Could it be that your faith is on trial (I Peter 1:7)? The context here is that I am not here to stay. Your thoughts have to be *I am going through* (passing through)! I'm going through something but I'm not staying here!

Your hope must be intensified in this trial. Hope turns your attitude and causes you to rise above where you are. You must pick up your visions and the things God has given you to do. You can't remain aimless. God has an answer for the aimlessness, and that's vision and purpose. Stand up and pick up your vision. Declare your purpose. God will make the way for you! It's a curse to live a life going nowhere. God has put you in this circumstance with hope. He's allowed this to intensify your hope! Why, my soul, are you downcast? Why so disturbed within me? Put your hope in God, for I will yet praise Him, my Savior, and my God (Psalm 42:5 KJV).

Without a doubt, He's got to make a way for you and me. You will not give up! Keep looking for it! Keep looking for it to change! Keep looking for God to make a way in a dead situation! Though it were dead, yet shall it live again! Don't stop looking! Don't give up! It's still to come! Say, I will get it! God promised it! I will get what God said!

DAY TWENTY JOURNALING

"Why art thou cast down, O my soul? And why art thou disquieted in me? Hope thou in God: for I shall yet praise Him, who is the health of my countenance, and my God." Psalm 42:5 KJV

DAY TWENTY-ONE - BE STILL AND KNOW

There are times in our lives when God may require that you quiet yourself in order to hear from Him. Life can be chaotic, and the trials of life can be overwhelming. Nonetheless, in the word of God, we find the prescription. "Be still, and know that I am God; I will be exalted among the nations" (Psalm 46:10 KJV). It's time to know that we are not in control of what happens in our lives. God does, however, want to reveal Himself in our situations. When God is exalted, it means others see Him by what He has allowed to happen in your life.

Being still means resting in who He is and not fretting because manifestation has not come yet. It means knowing as well as declaring, He's still got time! He has not forgotten about me! When we understand that He is bigger than any situation, we understand there is nothing too hard for Him.

He says, "Behold, I am the LORD, the God of all flesh: is there anything too hard for me" (Jeremiah 32:27 KJV)? If you are reading this, stop and think about the question. God is asking you, is there anything too hard for me? What is your response?

Events and situations give you history with God. He allows certain situations to arise so that He can stand up in them. He creates situations for revelation. So, in your stillness look for God in it. Listen for His voice. It doesn't matter how bad it looks, if there is a word from the Lord, it has to come forth! Your situation has to change! It has to happen! Do you believe it?

We can *know* Him by having an intimate relationship with Him. This is done by having a healthy prayer life. And by getting to know Him through and by what He says (in His Holy Word, the Bible), recognizing the things He does in our lives, and by way of His Spirit does He transform us from the inside out. God says be still and know for a reason. He says *be still* because when there is a lot going on you can't hear Him. When He says *know that I am God* it's because manifestation may not come right away. There may be no indication that you are coming out of the situation. But, when you really know God, no matter how long the wait, you know He's coming! When you really walk with Him, you know that His promises are yes and amen! In Numbers 23:19 we find this report, "God is not a man that He should lie; neither the son of man that He should repent: hath He said, and shall He not do it? Or hath He spoken, and shall He not make it good?" (KJV).

DAY TWENTY-ONE JOURNALING

_____

_____

_____

_____

_____

_____

_____

_____

_____

_____

_____

_____

_____

_____

"Be still and know that I am God; I will be exalted among the nations, I will be exalted in the earth." Psalm 46:10 NIV

DAY TWENTY-TWO - THE VOICE OF GOD

In the times we live in it's critical to know the voice of God. To know God's voice, one must spend time with Him in prayer and reading God's word (Bible). In the word of God, we find it duly noted as follows, "And when he putteth forth His own sheep, He goeth before them, and the sheep follow Him: for they know His voice. And a stranger will they not follow, but will flee from him: for they know not the voice of strangers (St. John 10:4-5 KJV). In these verses, we see that Jesus goes before the sheep. The sheep represent (us) His people. It lets us know that we don't know the way to go but He does. It also shows us the importance of Him leading the way.

Still, we notice that in order to follow Him they *must know* His voice. And how do they know His voice? Somewhere, and at some point, they've been around Him enough and gotten to know the sound of His voice. It's the same with us, we must spend time in God's presence so that we recognize His voice. I reiterate this happens in prayer and by the reading of God's word.

Additionally, a stranger is someone they don't know and are not familiar with. They flee strange people, places, and things. It means they run away from it because they sense danger. It's very important to know that we belong to God in every way. The scripture puts it this way, "Know ye that the LORD He is God: it is He that hath made us, and not we ourselves; we are His people, and the sheep of His pasture" (Psalm 100:3 KJV). Keeping in alignment with this thought it would make sense that you know God's voice because you belong to Him. He is very protective of His sheep. As you walk closely with God and develop your relationship with Him, this will be easy.

DAY TWENTY-TWO JOURNALING

_____

_____

_____

_____

_____

_____

_____

_____

_____

_____

_____

_____

"And when He putteth forth his own sheep, He goeth before them, and the sheep follow Him: for they know His voice. And a stranger will they not follow, but will flee from him: for they know not the voice of strangers." John 10:4-5 KJV

DAY TWENTY-THREE - WALK WORTHY

Walking with God requires a certain standard of living. It means living a life that represents Him. It means living a life that reflects His character. It means that God is counting on the investment He has made in you. He's expecting a return. Walking worthy means that God has sanctified (set apart) you for His use only. Without a doubt, this is true because Jesus died for you and shed His blood on the cross. His shed blood was the ransom used not only to forgive your sins but to make you righteous in Him. The scripture that comes to mind as I write this passage is found in I Thessalonians 4:4 KJV. It states, "That every one of you should know how to possess his own vessel in sanctification and honor."

Sanctification is what God has called you to. Your role in what He has done for you is for you to live your life according to the will of God. This may be something you are unfamiliar with and will need to learn about through the studying of God's word. It requires learning through and by engaging in Bible study and prayer, along with fasting. These are all spiritual exercises that strengthen you in your walk with God.

Still, there is a level of consecration required in this role for Christ-like living. A consecrated life is to live a holy life that is sacrificial in nature. It means letting go of some people, places, and things because you represent God. A vessel of honor is what God is looking for. In scripture, we see that it says, "Therefore, if anyone cleanses himself from what is dishonorable, he will be a vessel for honorable use, set apart as holy, useful to the master of the house, ready for every good work" (2 Timothy 2:21 ESV). Your perspective must change so that you see yourself as God sees you. You are a vessel chosen by God for God to accomplish His purpose in the earth. Remember, you're not just any vessel but an honorable one or God would not have selected you.

Think about it. He could have chosen anyone, but He chose you to put on display. The word honor means distinct, privileged, high respect, and to be esteemed. What an honor to be viewed by God in this way!

DAY TWENTY-THREE JOURNALING

_____

_____

_____

_____

_____

_____

_____

_____

_____

_____

_____

_____

_____

"That each of you should know how to possess his own vessel in sanctification and honor." I Thessalonians 4:4 KJV

DAY TWENTY-FOUR - BE NOT WEARY

One of the experiences that happens in our walk with God, while on this journey, is that we become weary. Weariness is feeling or showing tiredness, especially as a result of excessive exertion. This can happen to anyone who has walked with the Lord for any length of time. Perhaps God has not answered you as you expected Him to. Maybe you've spent years asking, seeking, and petitioning God. You might even think God has forgotten what He said to you. I am certain you've watched others who don't appear as dedicated to serving Christ as you are but are being blessed all around you. Still, you've prayed and seem to get no results. You've watched others get delivered by God, as a result of your prayers for them. I am sure you are asking yourself right about now, what is really going on?

You must always remember whenever you are going through any type of trial you can find comfort in the word of God (Bible). The scripture leaves us this encouragement, "And let us not therefore be not weary in well doing: for in due season we shall reap, if we faint not" (Galatians 6:9 KJV). We dealt with weariness, now let's deal with faintness and what this means. When one becomes faint, it happens in two ways. The first way is when things become unclear to the point of being barely perceptible. It's when movement is not seen, nor can it be detected or noticed. The second way is when you experience times of spiritual unconsciousness. This spiritual unconsciousness is when you are totally unaware of what God is doing in your life. More specifically, it's those times when it appears that even God is not aware of or not concerned with what is happening to you or around you. It's when your natural mind can't perceive the spiritual things of God.

Certainly, this scripture was left for us because God foreknew what we would experience and how exhausted we would become. However, quitting is not an option if you plan to see your due season. Understand what's being said here, you have a due season. It means at this time, on this particular day, God is going to bring you out!

Without a doubt, what is needed until your due season arrives is patience. Patience is the capacity to accept or tolerate delay, trouble, or suffering without getting angry or upset. I know many people find this hard and quite challenging. Nonetheless, if you've found yourself getting angry or even upset just ask the Savior to help you. Remember what the scripture says in Habakkuk 2:3 KJV, "For the vision *is* yet for an appointed time, but at the end it shall speak, and not lie: though it tarry, wait for it; because it will surely come, it will not tarry."

DAY TWENTY-FOUR JOURNALING

_____

_____

_____

_____

_____

_____

_____

_____

_____

_____

_____

_____

_____

"Let us not therefore be weary of well doing: for in due season we shall reap, if we faint not." Galatians 6:9 KJV

DAY TWENTY-FIVE - WHAT GOD ALLOWS

Have you ever been disappointed by what God allowed? You know, those times when you say to God or think to God, *God you knew this was going to happen, why didn't you stop it?* The unexplained trials, the unexplained disappointments, the unexplained waiting(s), all can leave you scratching your head. Life experiences can leave you baffled by what God allows. I mean really what do you say to God when He doesn't make sense? He's the creator of all life. The earth is His, the world, and they that dwell therein. What do say when you can't understand Him? God has given one diagnosis about Himself when He declares in scripture, "For my thoughts *are* not your thoughts, neither *are* your ways my ways, saith the LORD" (Isaiah 55:8 KJV).

The thing about living for Christ is that you don't belong to you and your life is not at all about you. Your life is about God's purpose, being carried out through you, while you reside on planet earth. We can only find solace when we understand this. I think we might be disappointed less often if we'd seek to align ourselves with the plan and will of God. I know, I know, it's easier said than done. Sometimes you may not want to do the will of God. Sometimes you're not feeling this God thing. There is one great reality and it's that God knew where you'd be, how you'd feel, and He has provided you with a way to deal with those times. What a mighty God we serve!

DAY TWENTY-FIVE JOURNALING

_____

_____

_____

_____

_____

_____

_____

_____

_____

_____

_____

_____

_____

_____

"For my thoughts are not your thoughts, neither are your ways my ways, saith the LORD." Isaiah 55:8 KJV

DAY TWENTY-SIX - RENEW YOUR MIND

The importance of a renewed mind is a critical element in our walk with God. The reason it's so critical is because our minds control us. The role that thinking plays in our lives can alter our destiny. Romans 12:2 KJV says, "And be not conformed to this world: but be ye transformed by the renewing of your mind, that ye may prove what is that good and acceptable will of God." It means that we are not to accept the way of the world. We are not to be influenced by the norms in this society, which typically permit us to do whatever our minds tell us to do. The world has its' standards, but we have been given a Holy standard according to the word of God. We are to be influenced by Him only.

The transformation component involves change. We read in the word of God, "Therefore, if any man *be* in Christ, *he is* a new creature: old things are passed away;

behold, all things are become new" (2 Corinthians, 5:17 KJV). So, everything about you should be new and this includes your mind. The change of mind demonstrates that you are capable of living according to God's plan for your life. And this pleases Him. Notwithstanding, others will see the transforming power of God, through your life and desire salvation. We are living epistles read and known of men (2 Corinthians, 3:2 KJV).

One of the most challenging ways of thinking about your life is that you are not of this world. I know, it's hard to understand. This is why it's imperative to be transformed by the renewing of your mind so that you can understand this way of thinking. If you have given your life to Christ on any level, you are not the norm. You don't fit in. You will stick out like a sour thumb. And quite frankly, you will not be received. This is true because Jesus Christ had the same experience on earth. God left an explanation when He said, "If the world hate you, ye know that it hated me before it hated you. If ye were of the world, the world would love his own: but because ye are not of the world, but I have chosen you out of the world, therefore the world hateth you" (St. John 15:18-19 KJV).

As you continue to walk with God just know that there will be a constant battle between your natural man and your spiritual man. The old ways of thinking, believing, responding, and living will try to return. Still, as you learn how to possess this new life in Christ Jesus, things will become a bit easier. You will soon learn how to get rid of thoughts that are intrusive and that try to invade your mind. You'll learn how to meditate on God's word so that you can combat anything contrary to what He has spoken to you. Something that you will need to be conscious and intentional about is found in (2 Corinthians 10:5). "We demolish arguments and every pretension that sets itself up against the knowledge of God and we take captive every thought to make it obedient to Christ." Beloved, what this means is that you eliminate all opposing thoughts that don't align themselves with the word of God. Specifically, this means that you keep away from the thoughts that make you think contrary to what God has commanded in your life. Remember, it is your personal experience with God that no one can take from you. Not even the devil! Whenever you began to think something that's not right, acknowledge it and began to declare out loud what God has said to you about this. This will come more naturally as you study the word of God and become familiar with the voice and thoughts of God. I reiterate studying the Bible because you will experience mental attacks from the enemy.

One final concern about thoughts. They can become your reality. It may seem strange, but thoughts are connected to your heart. What's in your heart will manifest in your speech and eventually, you will say it and your ears will hear it. This is what you must be careful of. There is a portion in scripture that says, "For as he thinketh in his heart, so is he" (Proverbs 23:7 KJV). In other words, what you think in your heart is who you are. I strongly encourage you to meditate on the word of God that you might not sin against God. When you do this, you begin to speak into existence what God has spoken to you. So, you'll learn how to do this exercise without thinking about it. It will become second nature as you will find yourself doing it in every area of your life. Try it!

DAY TWENTY-SIX JOURNALING

_____

_____

_____

_____

_____

_____

_____

_____

_____

_____

_____

_____

"And be not conformed to this world: but be ye transformed by the renewing of your mind, that ye may prove what is that good, and acceptable, and perfect will of God." Romans 12:2 KJV

DAY TWENTY-SEVEN - ORDER MY STEPS

Our steps can lead us to many places. Sometimes we know the way, then there are other times in life we really don't know the way. This is precisely why we should ask for guidance from our heavenly father. In the book of Psalm 23:3 YLT, we can see the behavior of our shepherd. In this verse it says, "My soul He refresheth; He leadeth me in the paths of righteousness, for His name's sake." What this lets us know is that there are times when we need to be brought back to a certain place and this can't be done by our own volition. It's when we need the guidance of the shepherd. In this case, it's Jesus who is our shepherd.

In order to understand the concept of a shepherd and a shepherd's importance in your life, you must first know why you need a shepherd. The text used it as an analogy to show the role of God in our lives. And it also shows us what we mean to Him. It reveals how dependent we should be on

Him for guidance and direction. It explains that sheep don't know the right (righteousness) paths to take.

In the real world, sheep require a shepherd because they really don't know where to go. They require guidance from their shepherd. They can't keep themselves from hurt, harm, or danger. Sheep by nature are very dependent animals. They are trained to respond only to their shepherd's voice and will not respond to a stranger. In actuality, they are known to become startled by unfamiliar voices. Likewise, we find a scripture that speaks to this. It says, "And a stranger will they not follow, but will flee from him: for they know not the voice of strangers" (St. John 10:5 KJV).

The key is to remember that the shepherd always knows what's best and provides for His sheep as He sees fit. In this aspect, we are His sheep and the sheep of His pasture. He wants to provide for us in every area of our lives. He wants to direct our paths. The word says, "In all thy ways acknowledge Him, and He shall direct thy paths" (Proverbs 3:6 KJV). We only need to go to Him; know His voice; and listen when He speaks. Once we learn the voice of God anything else that is contrary to it must be ignored. When He gives you instruction you've got to know that it's for your good. It's because He knows the end from the beginning. He sees for us. He keeps us from the predator. He keeps us from the destroyer of our souls. A word of caution here is that you will be eaten by a predator if you don't listen and obey God.

DAY TWENTY-SEVEN JOURNALING

_____

_____

_____

_____

_____

_____

_____

_____

_____

_____

_____

_____

_____

_____

"He restoreth my soul; He leadeth me in the paths of righteousness for His name's sake." Psalm 23:3 KJV

DAY TWENTY-EIGHT - HOW TO PROSPER

In 3 John 1:2, John is praying according to the will of God. He's praying that in *all* things we are prosperous. The *all* here represents variations of all (i.e. different types) of prosperity. God wants you to be in health. That's physical. God wants you healthy! God wants you prosperous! Keep in mind this prosperity is in proportion to your soul prospering. This soul prosperity has to do with Jesus. This happened when Jesus died on the cross.

Our physical health is tied up with our soul's prosperity. Even our prosperity on earth is tied up with our soul's prosperity. God wants us to prosper in every area in all respects. Here is where the will of God for how this happens can throw some people off. How God chooses to prosper some may not be how He chooses to prosper you. This is something to grapple with because for some it comes easier than for others as you look from the outside in.

Joshua 1:8 KJV says, "This book of the law shall not depart from your mouth; but thou shall meditate therein day and night, that thou mayest observe to do according to all that is written therein: for then thou shall make thy way prosperous, and then thou shalt have good success."

In the word of God, we find that we have to meditate on it day and night. In the word of God, we must carefully obey it. Please know that this won't come easy. It will require discipline and being intentional about your time spent with God in His presence. Life will still happen as you attempt to obey the word of God. It's really going to be the spiritual exercises you do that will help you attain the desires and will of God for your life. I feel the need to reiterate and prepare you for the difficultly you should anticipate as you go after God. Expect the attack of the enemy on your mind; your body; your finances; and your will to serve God. Everything that you have believed to be true about your Savior will be tested! Nonetheless, it is God's will that you prosper in every area of your life.

DAY TWENTY-EIGHT JOURNALING

_____

_____

_____

_____

_____

_____

_____

_____

_____

_____

_____

_____

_____

_____

_____

_____

"Beloved, I wish above all things that thou mayest prosper and be in health, even as thy soul prospereth." 3 John 1:2 KJV

DAY TWENTY-NINE - THAT I MIGHT KNOW HIM

Some proclaim to know God. This is not something to be said or taken lightly. Knowing God comes through many trials and tribulations. Knowing Him *requires* great suffering. There is no other way to really know Christ. Suffering can happen and does happen at a moment's notice. Suffering has no respect of person. It's me today, but it could be you tomorrow. The thing about suffering is that when it's from God, we can't control how long it will be. He ultimately decides.

Through suffering, we learn more about ourselves and how much faith we truly have in our creator. Through suffering, we decide daily whether to keep the faith or throw in the towel. While in this place of suffering we have lots of reflection time, questioning time, and evaluating where we really are in Him versus where we think we are. In Philippians 3:10 KJV, it says, "That I may know him, and the power of His resurrection, and the fellowship of His sufferings, being made conformable unto His death." Here we see what knowing God truly means. It means not only sharing in His mighty power that raised Jesus from the dead but sharing in His death as well.

This literally means that death comes before resurrecting power! It really means dying to you, your ways, your ideologies, and what your plans are. It is not until something dies that resurrection power can be seen in your life. Dying is not easy because of the constant war that is going on between the Spirit and your flesh. Jesus puts it this way, "No man takes it from me, but I lay it down of myself. I have power to lay it down, and I have power to take it again. This commandment have I received of my Father" (St. John 10:18 KJV). This should be your posture as you come to know the Father. Lay down your life and you will see the resurrection power of Christ being made manifest in you.

DAY TWENTY-NINE JOURNALING

_____

_____

_____

_____

_____

_____

_____

_____

_____

_____

_____

_____

"That I may know Him, and the power of His resurrection, and the fellowship of His sufferings, being made conformable unto His death." Philippians 3:10 KJV

DAY THIRTY - PRAISE HIM

Praise Him! According to Psalm 150:6 KJV, the word encourages us, "Let everything that has breathe praise the LORD." Praise the LORD. This should be something that comes without reservation. But believe it or not, it doesn't. It can become hard to do if your perspective is flawed or on the wrong way of thinking. It's another spiritual exercise that you must train yourself to do. Praise is a form of salutation that acknowledges, as well as, compliments God.

We praise Him because of who He is. We praise Him for what He has done, will do, and always does. We praise Him because He's worthy of the praise. We praise Him because He deserves it. We praise Him because He commands us to do so. We praise Him because He's a loving heavenly father. We praise Him because of His goodness. We praise Him because of His tender mercies. We praise Him because He never sleeps nor slumbers. We praise Him because of His mighty acts. We praise Him for His loving kindness. We praise Him because His compassions fail not. We praise Him because His mercies are new every morning.

We praise Him because we have breath in our bodies. We praise Him because He's gracious. We praise Him because we have the activities of our limbs. We praise Him because there is blood still running warm in our veins. We praise Him because of His mighty acts. There are so many reasons to praise Him.

Take some time and practice praising Him. Think of times in which you are grateful and have seen the hand of God manifest in your life. You should not have to think very far. When you *think*, you will *thank*. Take my word for it, when you began to do this exercise on praise, you will feel better instantly. It's like the more you praise Him, here comes another thought of praise, and it keeps going and going.

DAY THIRTY JOURNALING

_____

_____

_____

_____

_____

_____

_____

_____

_____

_____

_____

_____

_____

_____

_____

"Let everything that has breath praise the LORD. Praise the LORD." Psalm 150:6 KJV

www.ingramcontent.com/pod-product-compliance
Lightning Source LLC
LaVergne TN
LVHW051249080426
835513LV00016B/1817